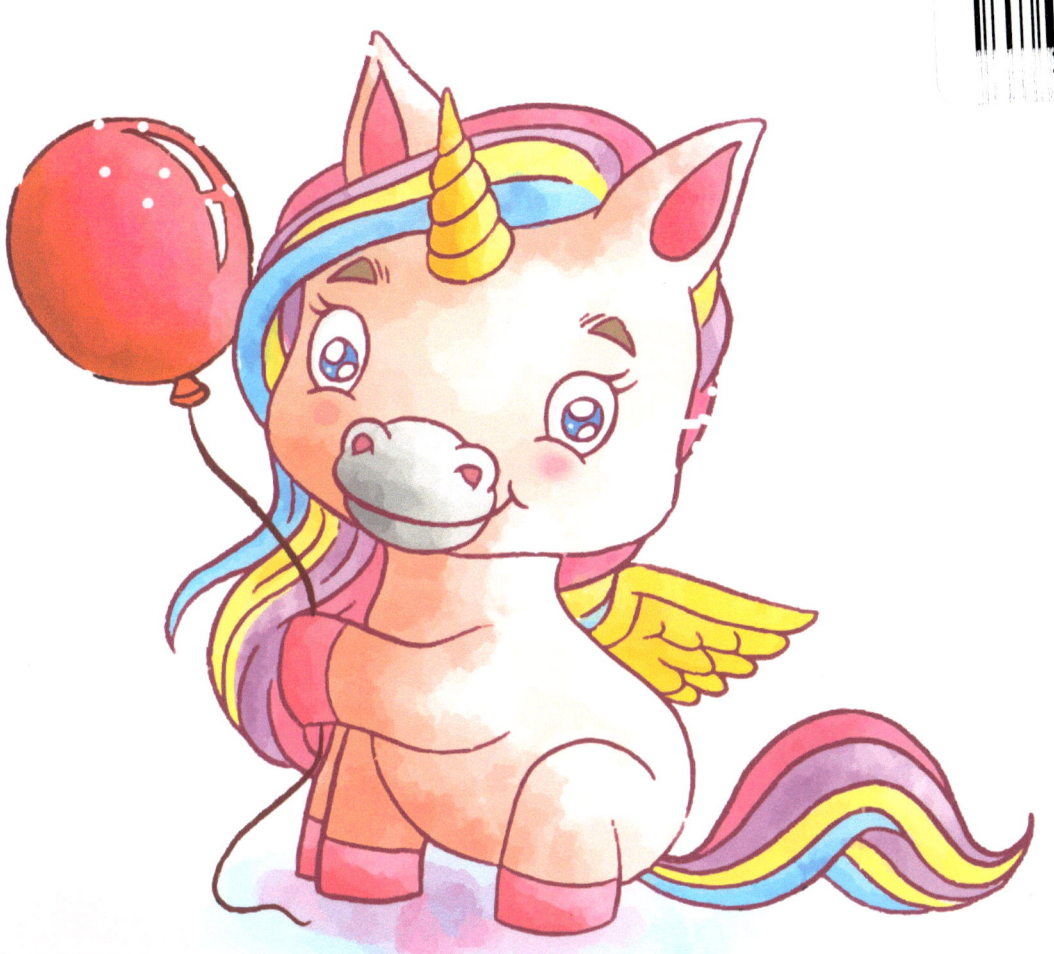

This coloring book belongs to:

....

Copyright | 2021 Aquarella Publishing

All rights reserved. No part of this publication may be reproduced, stored in a retrieval system, or transmitted, in any form or in any means – by electronic, mechanical, photocopying recording or otherwise – without prior written permission.

How to use this book

Painting is very therapeutic and stress relieving for kids, so this collection of cute designs is something that little animal lovers would love!

With this coloring book, you can follow the given colored example of each design with its color palette and try to reproduce it or you can let your imagination go wild and make your version. You can use watercolor markers, pencils, or paints.

The pages are single-sided to prevent bleed-through, they can be removed and displayed without losing any image on the back.

Even the paper of this book is of premium quality, and thick enough; it's better to place a piece of cardboard paper under the page while coloring to prevent any eventual unwanted bleed through and indents.

To use this book with watercolor paints in a more sophisticated way than traditional coloring sheets, It's recommended to print the practice pages on a thick, heavy watercolor paper so you can experience many colors and keep practicing as much as you want!

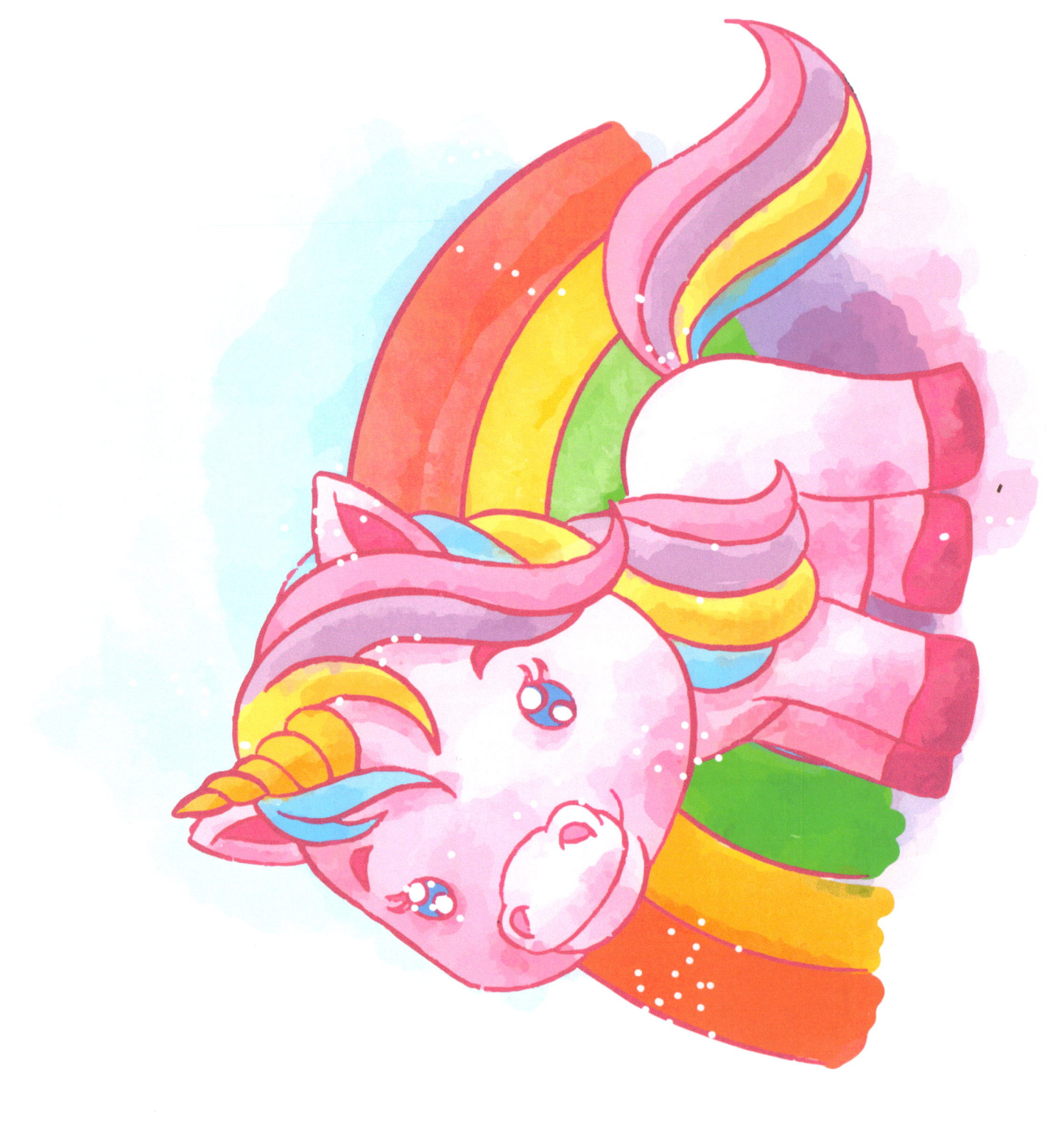

COLOR PALETTE

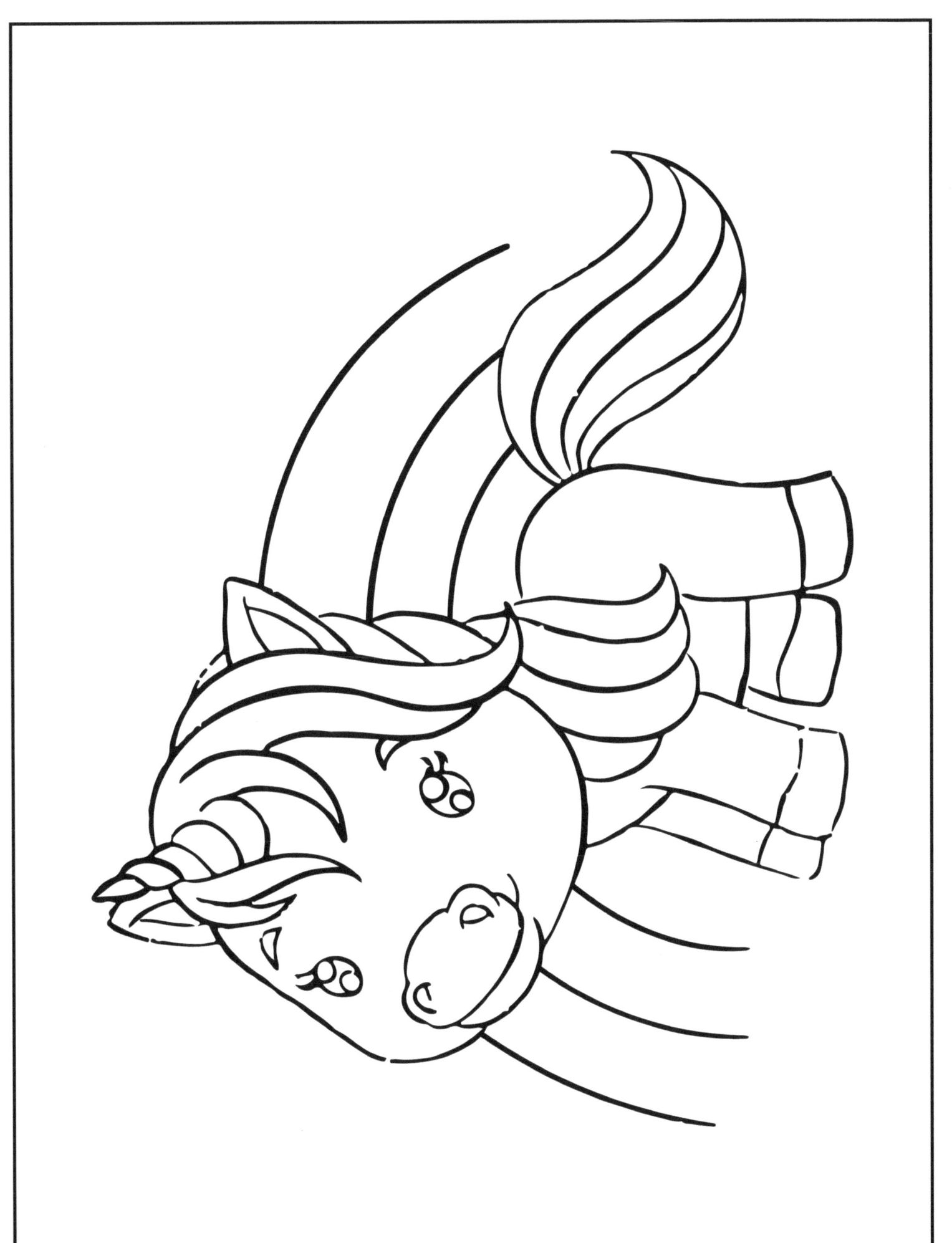

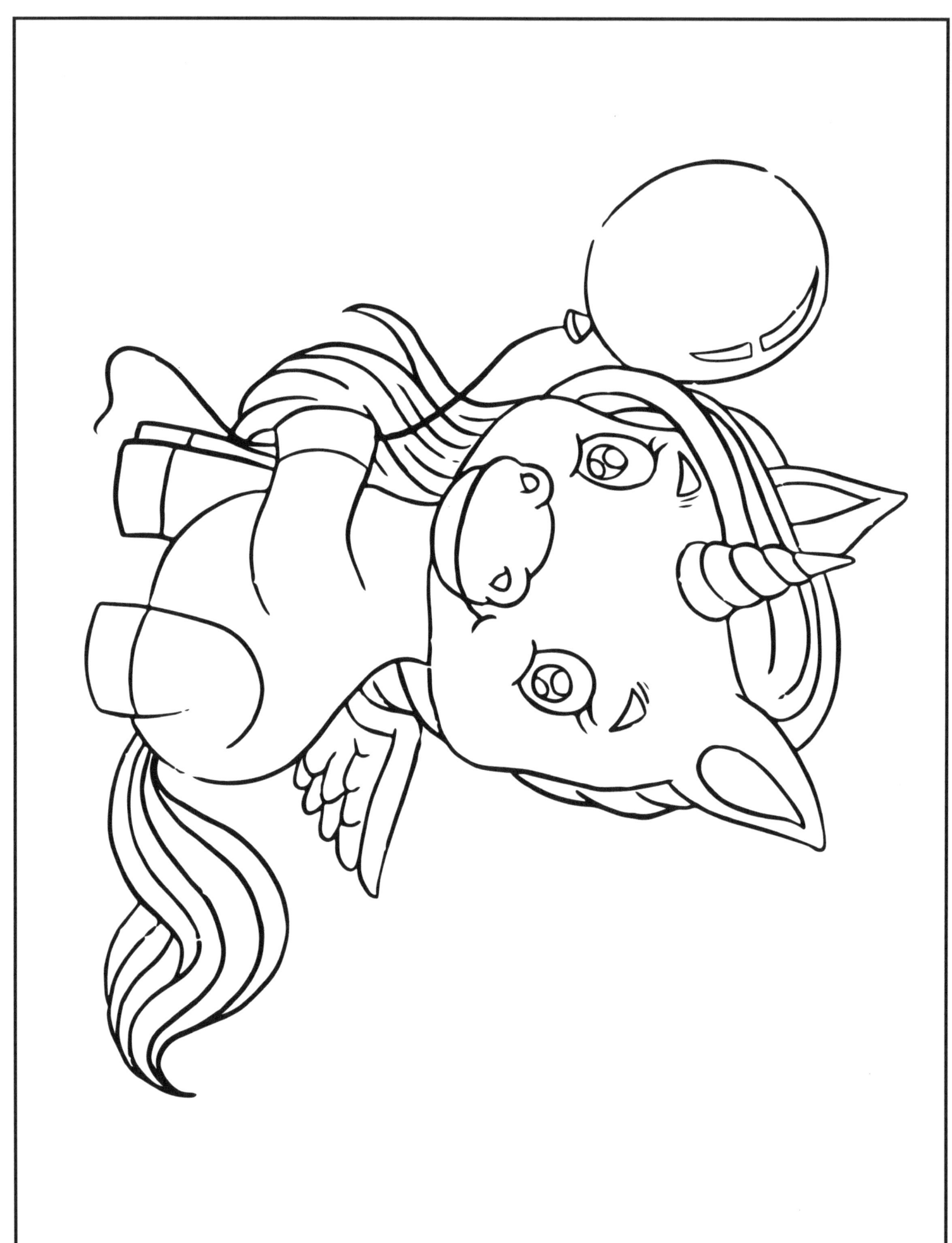

COLOR PALETTE

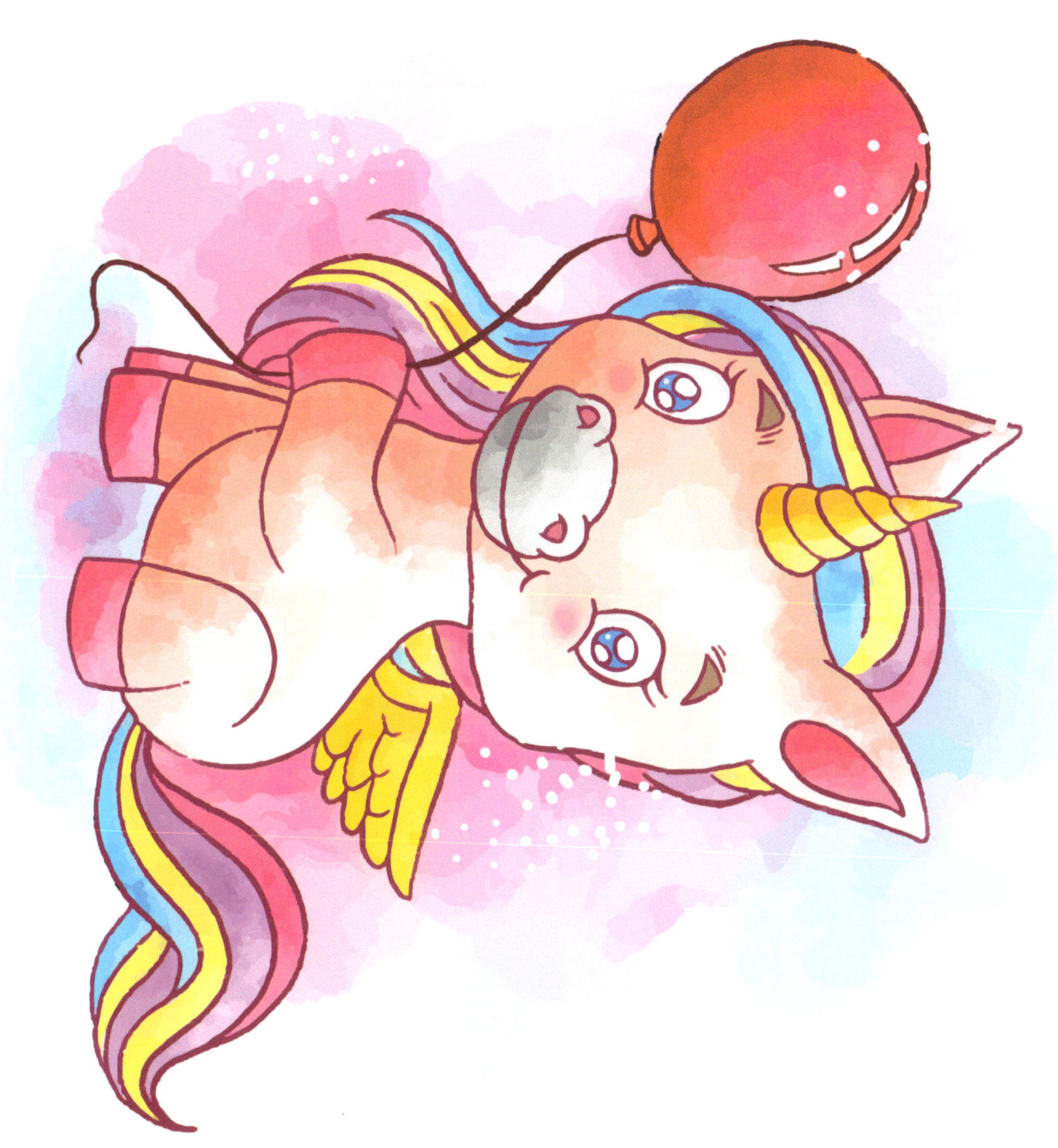

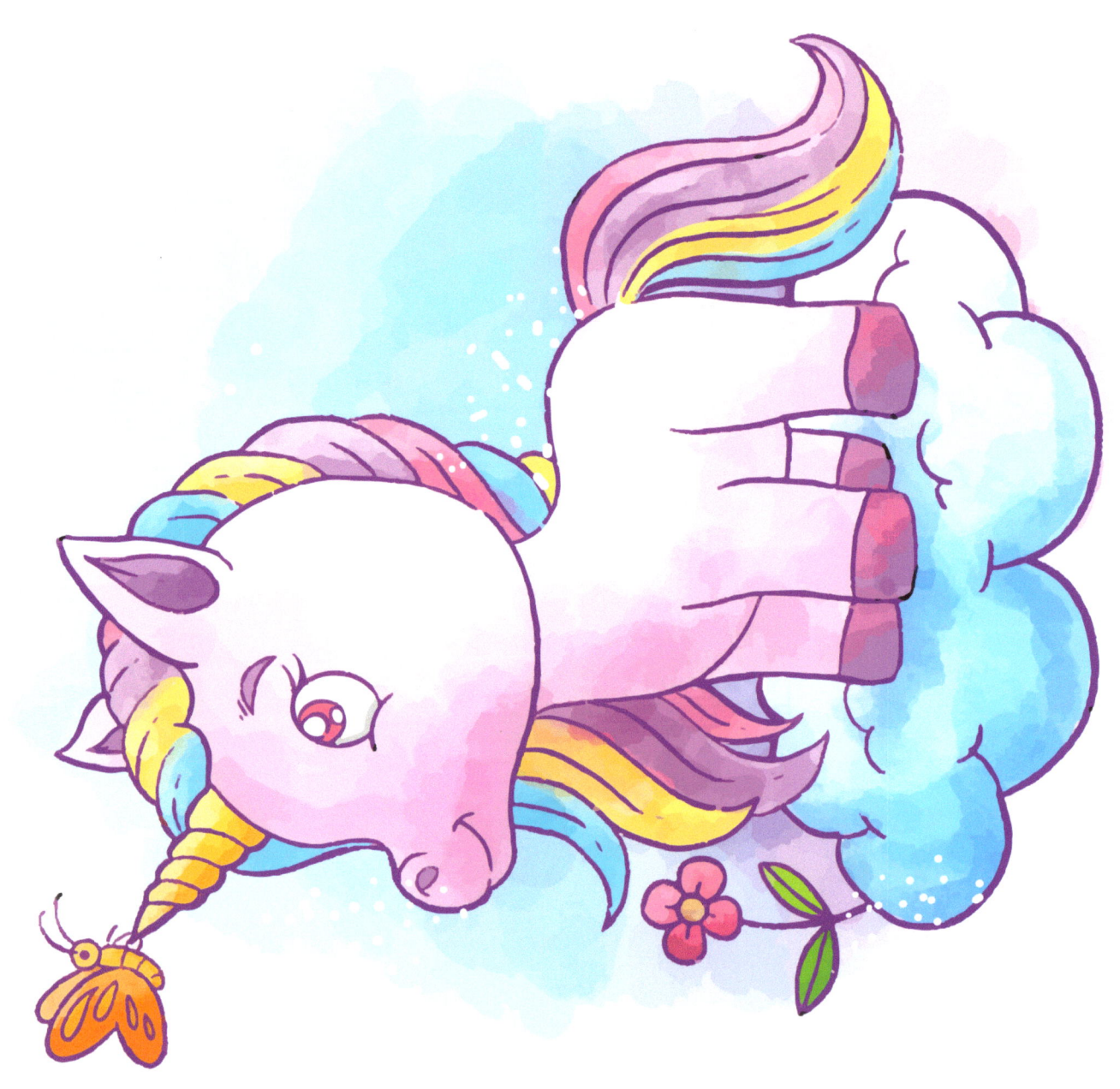

COLOR PALETTE

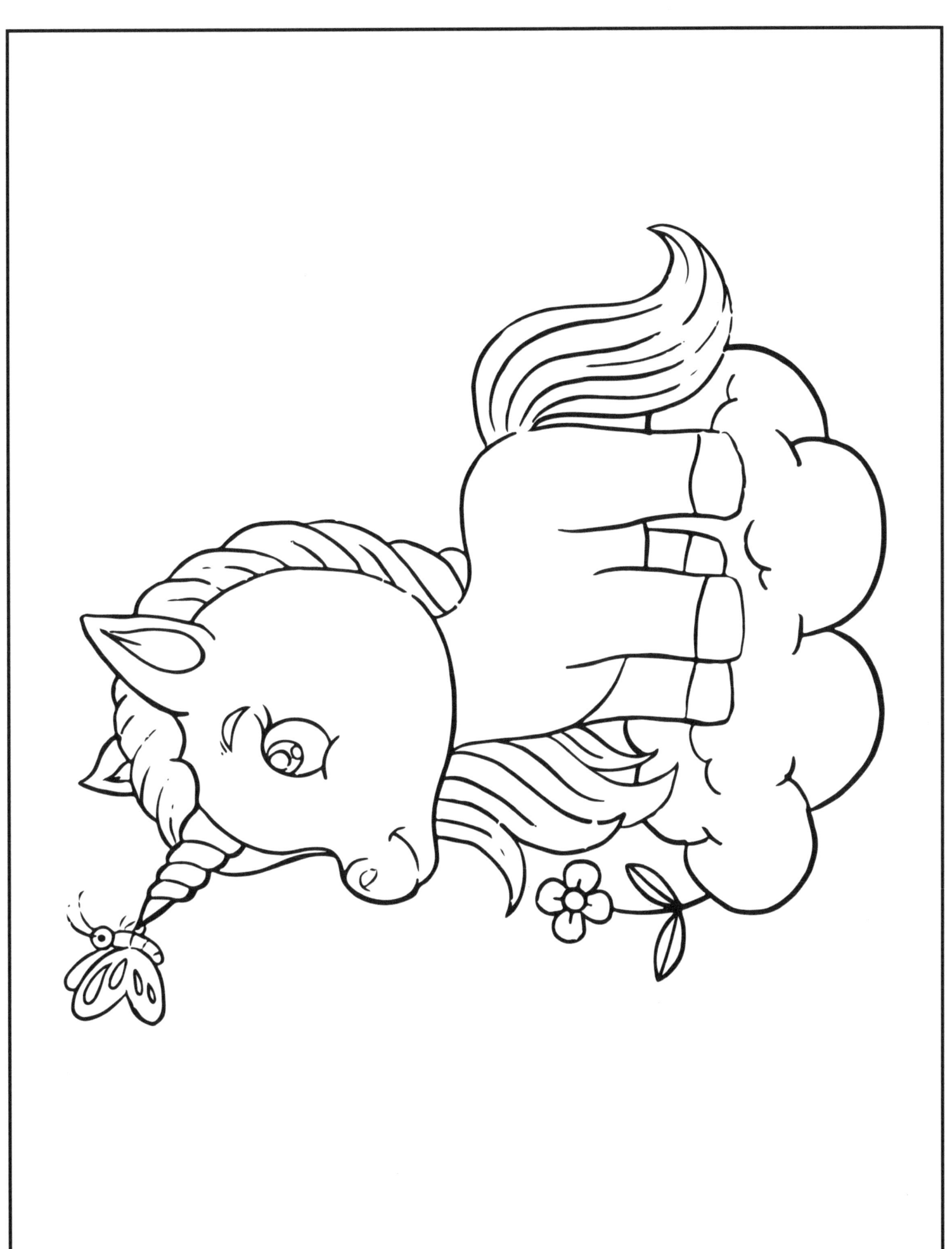

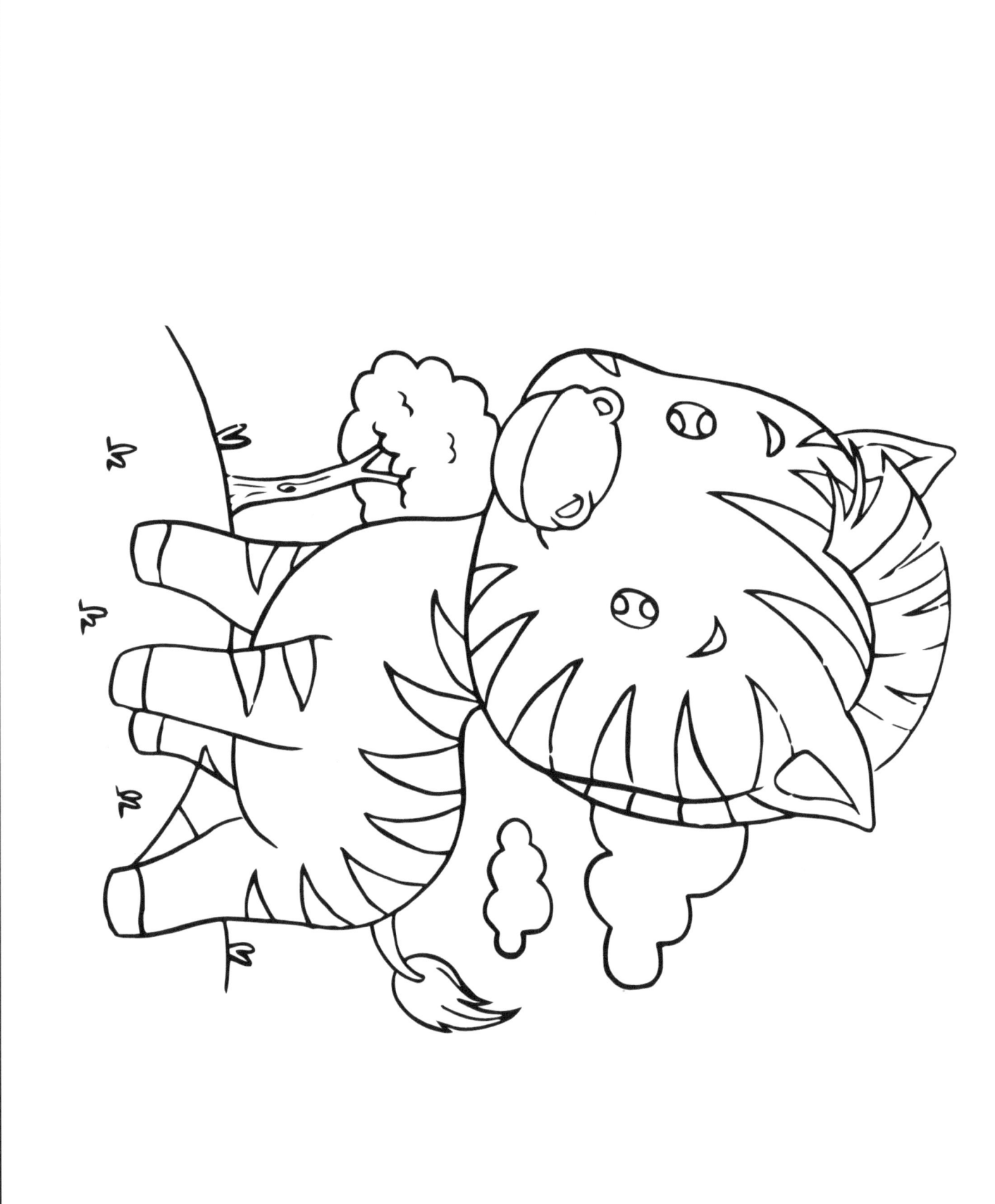

COLOR PALETTE

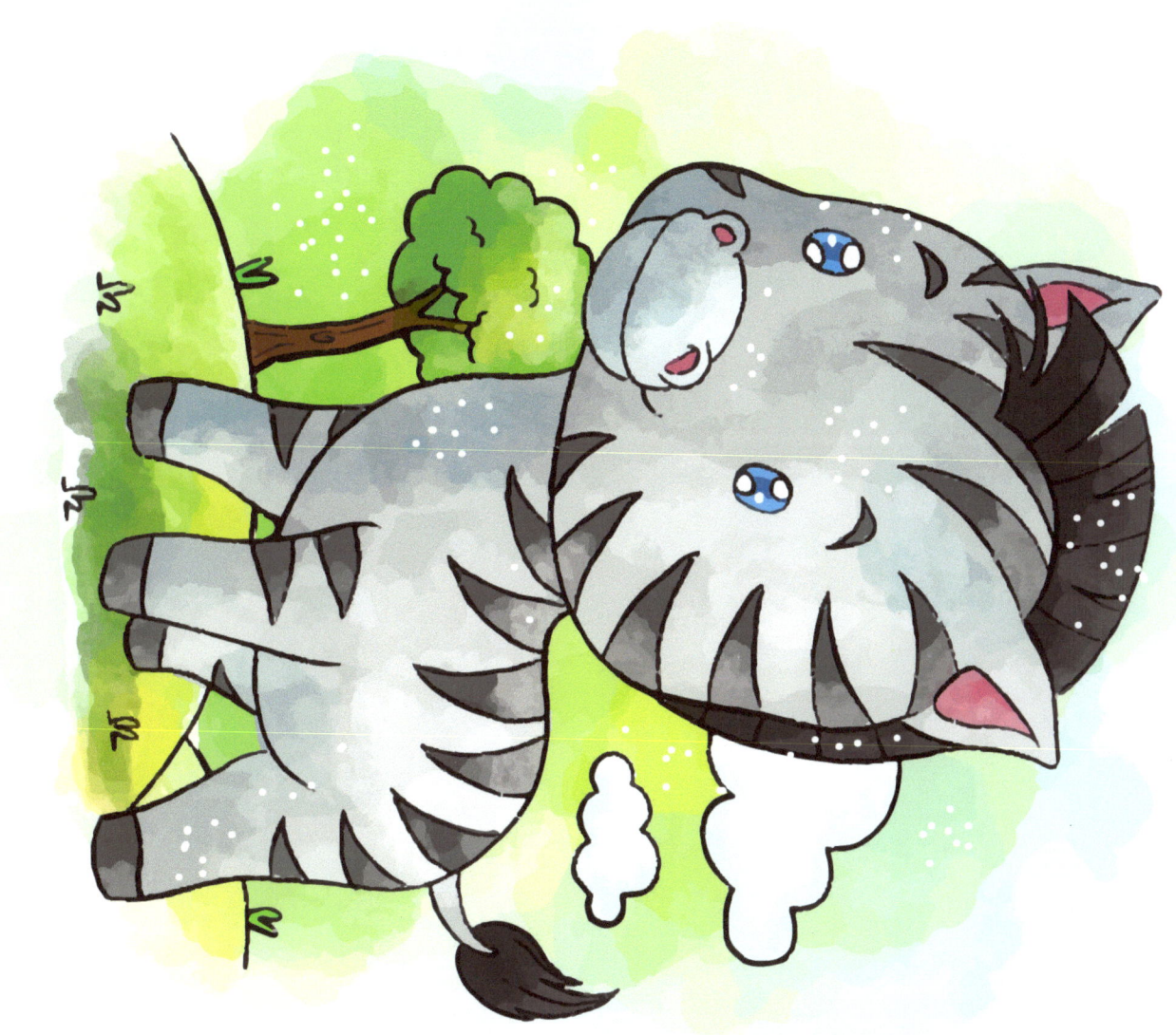

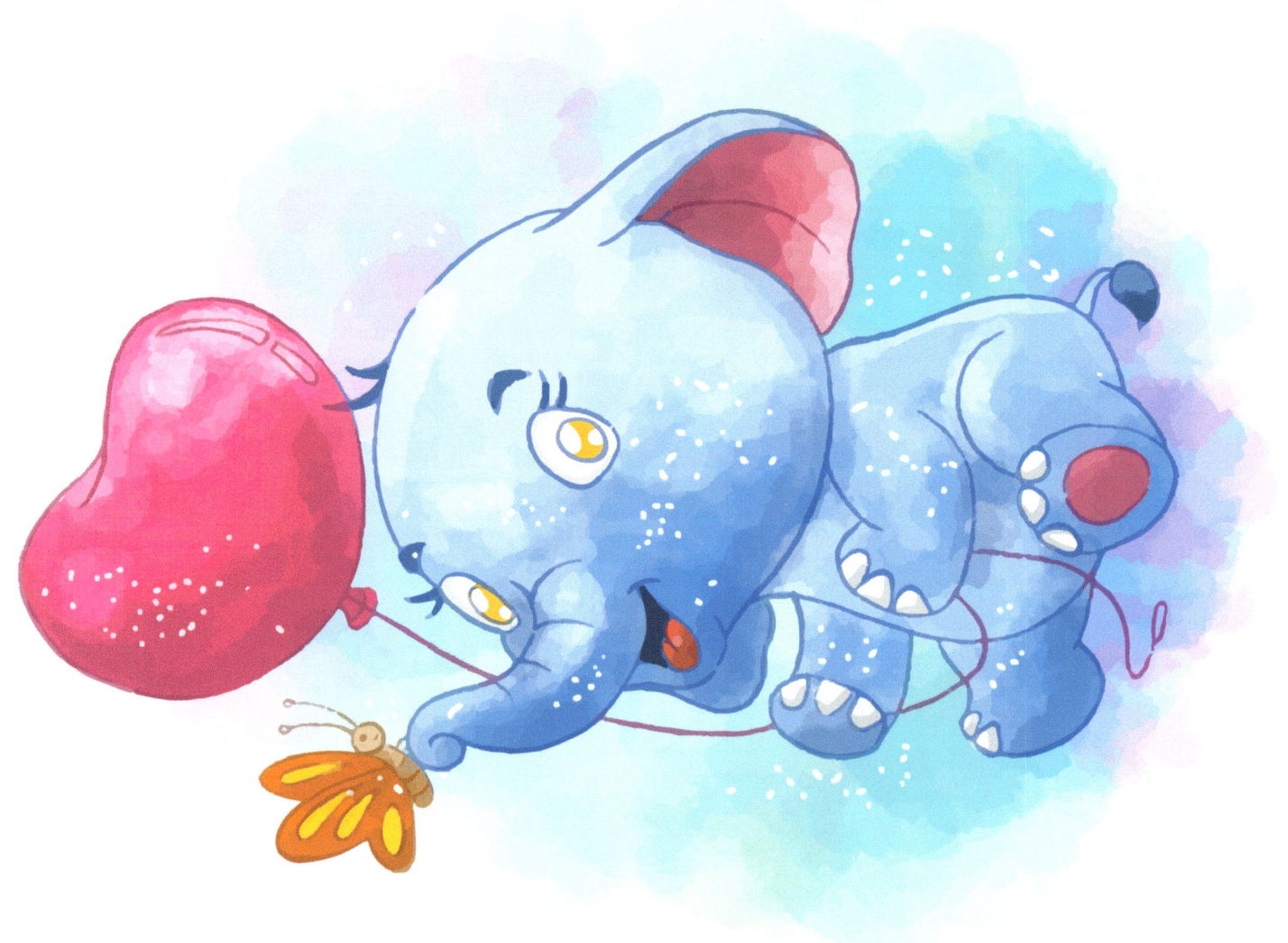

COLOR PALETTE

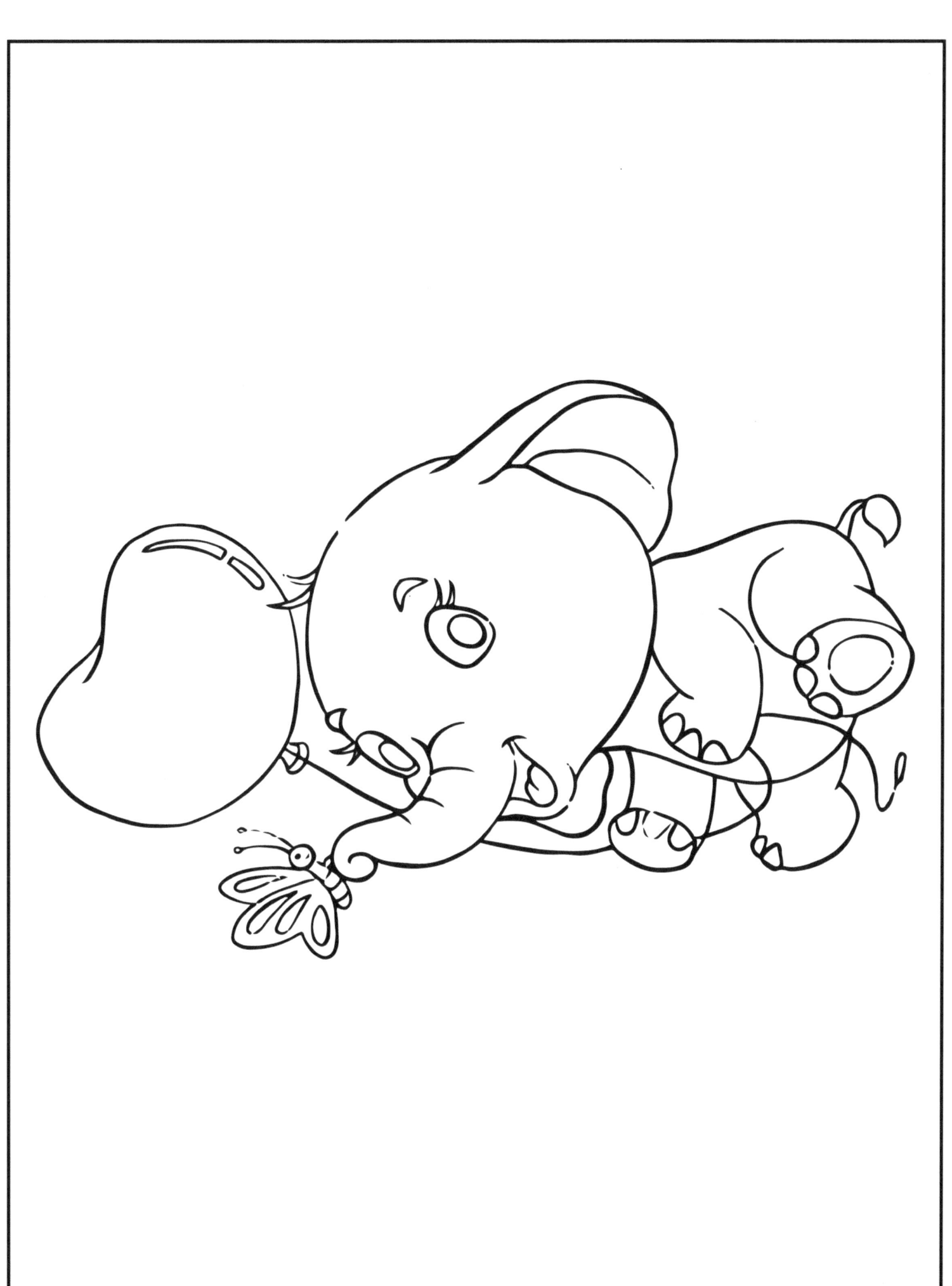

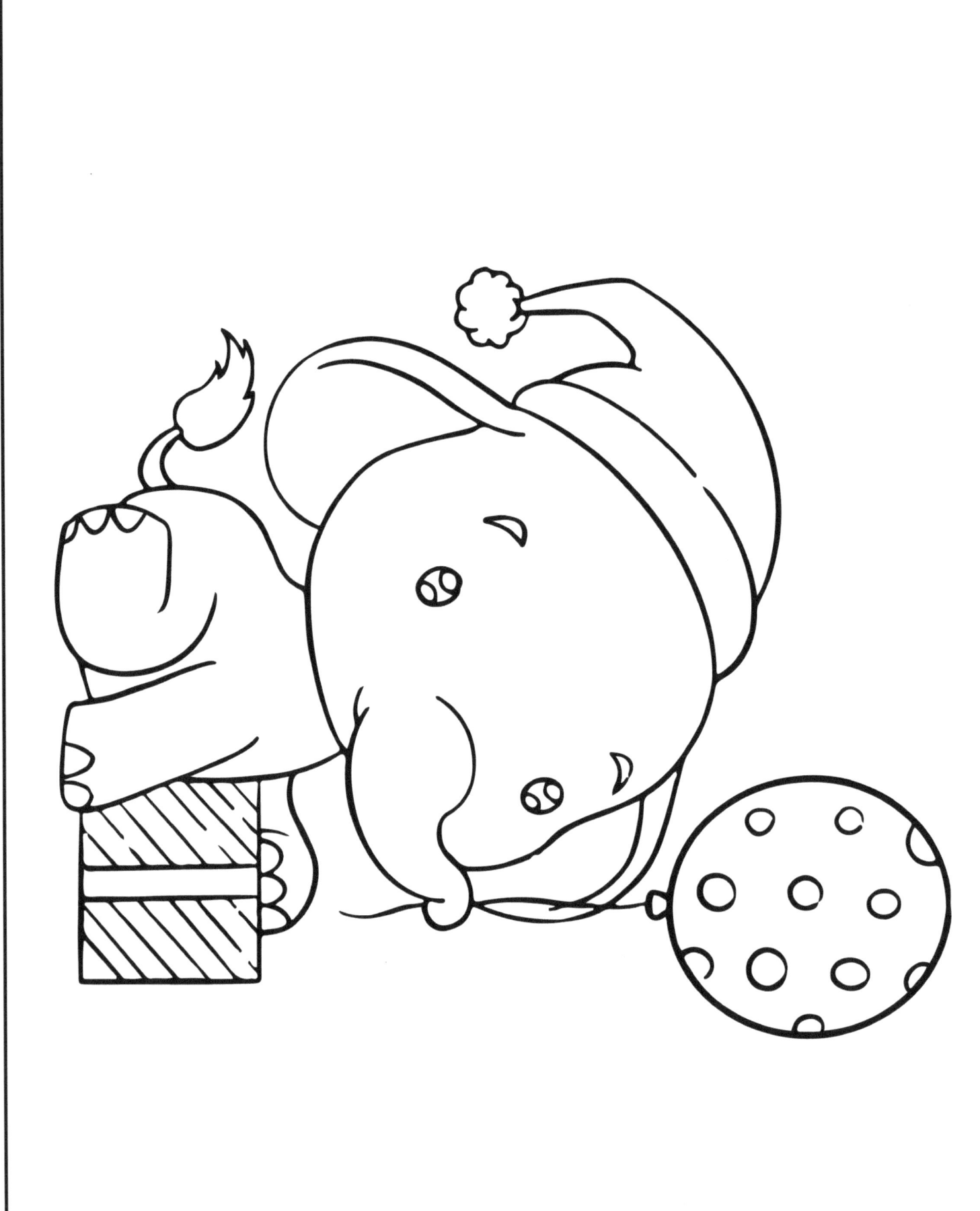

COLOR PALETTE

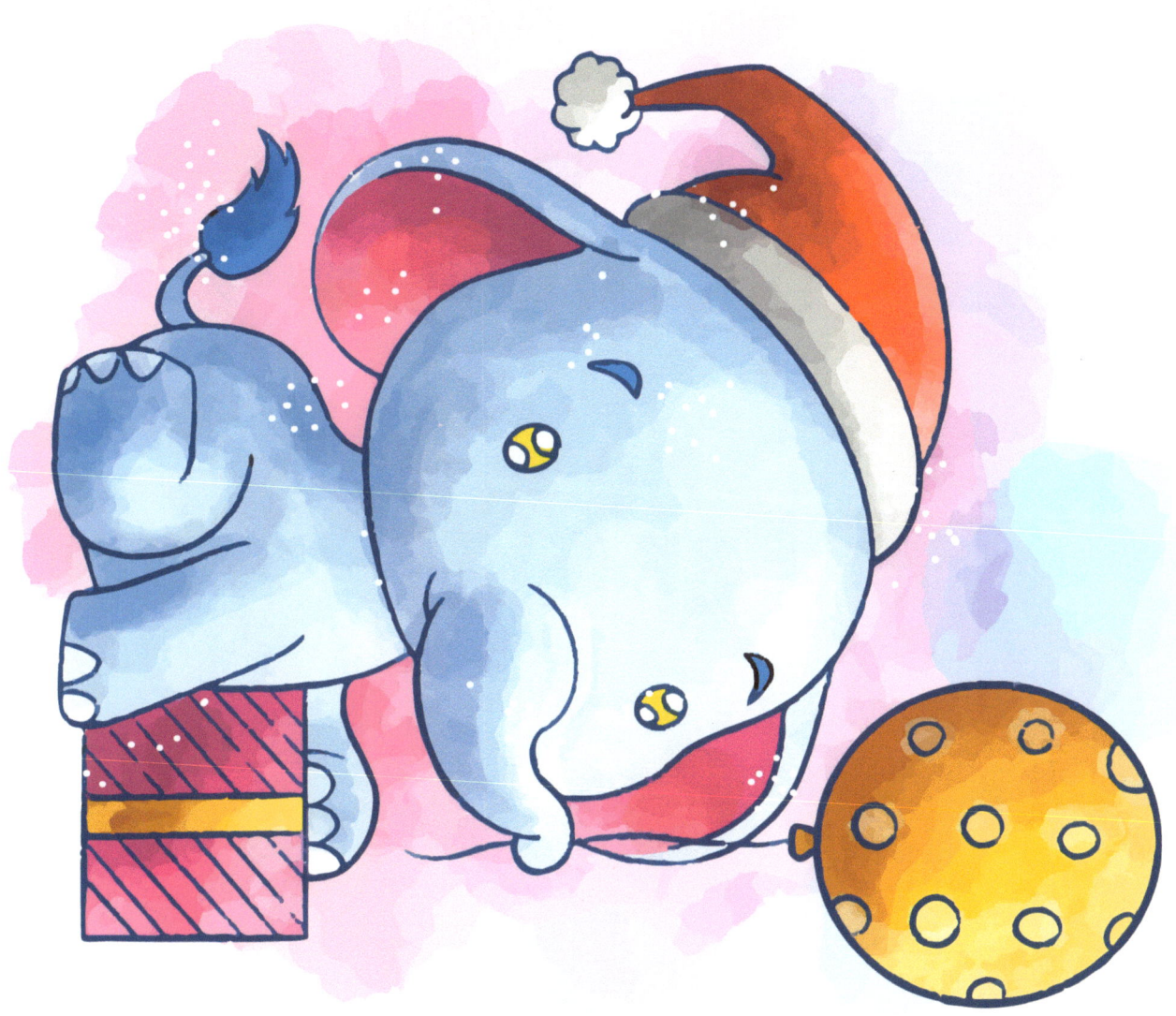

Do you want more?
Check this book

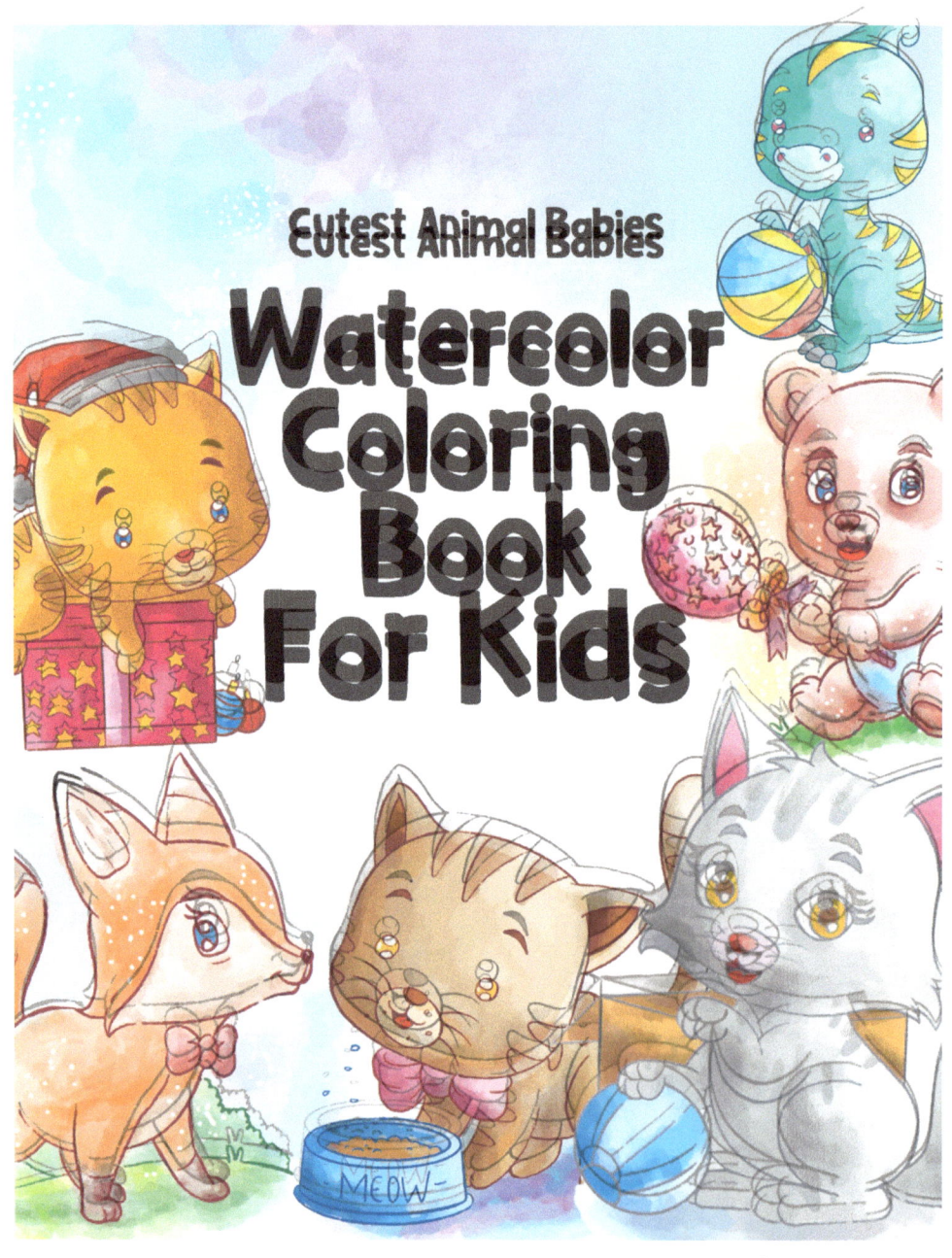

https://www.amazon.com/dp/B08XZQ826S

www.ingramcontent.com/pod-product-compliance
Lightning Source LLC
Chambersburg PA
CBHW051943210526
45473CB00006B/2364